W9-ADC-698

# TARA
# LIPINSKI

BY RICHARD RAMBECK

*(Photo on front cover)*

*USA's Tara Lipinski performs her routine at the White Ring Arena in Nagano, Japan. February 20, 1998.*

*(Photo on previous pages)*

*Gold medalist Tara Lipinski, center, silver medalist Michelle Kwan, left, and bronze medalist Vanessa Gusmeroli of France at the World Figure Skating Championships in Lausanne, Switzerland. March 22, 1997.*

**GRAPHIC DESIGN**
Robert A. Honey, Seattle

**PHOTO RESEARCH**
James R. Rothaus, James R. Rothaus & Associates

**ELECTRONIC PRE-PRESS PRODUCTION**
Robert E. Bonaker, Graphic Design & Consulting Co.

**PHOTOGRAPHY**
All photos by Associated Press AP

Library of Congress Cataloging-in-Publication Data
Rambeck, Richard
Tara Lipinski / by Richard Rambeck
p. cm.
Summary: A brief biography of the youngest skater ever to win United States and World Figure Skating Championships and go on to win a gold medal in the 1998 Winter Olympics.
ISBN 1-56766-525-5 (library : reinforced : alk. paper)

1. Lipinski, Tara, 1982- — Juvenile literature.
2. Skaters—United States—Biography—Juvenile literature.
[1. Lipinski, Tara 1982- . 2. Figure skaters. 3. Women—Biography.]
I. Title
GV850.J56R36 1998 98-6785
796.91'2'092 — dc21 CIP
[B] AC

# CONTENTS

*Tara Lipinski, flanked by her coaches Megan Faulkner, left, and Richard Callaghan, right, reacts to her scores in Nagano, Japan. Febuary 20, 1998.*

First Tara Lipinski cried, but just a little. Then she laughed—a lot. And then she screamed and jumped up and down. She kept on screaming and jumping. She was finally acting her age—like any 15-year-old girl who was very, very happy. But Tara Lipinski wasn't really like any other 15-year-old girl. Why not? Because she had just won a gold medal. In fact, she had just become the youngest figure skater ever to win an Olympic gold medal.

## HAPPY DAYS

Finally the screaming and the jumping stopped, but the smile didn't leave Lipinski's face for days. She had done what few people thought she could do. She had skated better than fellow American Michelle Kwan. Kwan, the experts said, would almost certainly win the gold medal at the 1998 Winter Olympics in Nagano, Japan. The experts thought Lipinski would probably get the silver. Lipinski didn't skate to win the gold medal. "I had to go out there and concentrate on my program, and not worry about winning or not," she said.

## THE DOOR LEFT OPEN

When Lipinski took the ice for her long program, she was in second place behind Kwan. Kwan had already skated her long program and had done well, but she hadn't been perfect. Kwan didn't fall, but some of her jumps weren't her best. Kwan, who had seemed unbeatable, had left the door open for Lipinski, but Lipinski needed to skate the performance of her life. The music—"The Rainbow"—began, and Lipinski started her program. Afterward, she admitted she was nervous at first. It took her one jump to lose that nervousness.

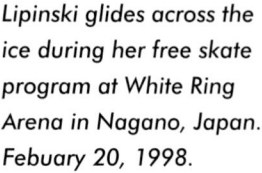

*Lipinski glides across the ice during her free skate program at White Ring Arena in Nagano, Japan. Febuary 20, 1998.*

*Lipinski celebrates after completing her free skate program in Nagano, Japan. Febuary 20, 1998.*

## TWO TRIPLE JUMPS

"After that first jump," Lipinski said, "I forgot about everything and just skated." She seemed to float on the ice and then fly above it on her jumps. The 80-pound Lipinski was like tissue paper in a gentle breeze. No women skater—not Kwan, not anybody else—jumped like Lipinski. About midway through the program, she did one triple jump, landed, and then did another triple jump right away. "She's the only one to do that," said Scott Hamilton, the 1984 men's Olympic gold medalist, "and she hits it every time."

## THE EXCITING END

Finally, after a few more jumps, all of them done perfectly, the program was over. Lipinski stood briefly at the center of the ice as the crowd roared its approval. Then she was off, practically running on her skates, waving her arms. She ran into the arms of her coach, Richard Callaghan. Lipinski was so relieved that her program was over, she

11

began to cry. Callaghan patted her on the back and told her she had skated wonderfully. Within seconds, Lipinski's tears were replaced by laughter. She looked into the television camera and wished a friend happy birthday. Then she waited to see her marks from the judges.

*Lipinski, front, Michelle Kwan, left, and Chen Lu, back, wave to the crowd as they make their way off the ice following the medal ceremony at the Nagano Olympic Games. Febuary 20, 1998.*

## THE GOLD MEDAL

As soon as the marks flashed on the scoreboard, Lipinski knew that she, and not Kwan, had won the gold. Then the screaming and jumping started. Later, Lipinski stood on the medals stand, received her gold, and listened to the playing of the U.S. national anthem. "It was amazing," she said of the medals ceremony. "It went by so quick. I couldn't think of anything wrong, I couldn't think of anything negative. Everything was perfect." Everything was indeed perfect for Lipinski, who became the youngest person ever to win a Winter Olympics gold medal in any individual sport.

*Lipinski was 13 years old when she skated in the U.S Figure Skating Championships on January 20, 1996. She placed third.*

## LIPINSKI'S DREAM

Tara Lipinski first dreamed of winning a gold medal when she was two years old. She watched the 1984 Summer Olympics, including the medals ceremonies, on television. Then she made her own medals platform and her own gold medal. She stood on the platform with her medal and imagined that someone had just handed her a bouquet of flowers. When she was nine, she was already a national roller skating champion. But her main sport was figure skating. Her family lived in Texas, but Lipinski and her mom moved to Detroit so she could train. Her father, Jack Lipinski, stayed in Texas.

## SIX HOURS A DAY

Every day, for six hours and sometimes more, Lipinski practiced. Despite all the skating, she was still able to have fun, to be a kid. "I missed a few birthday parties," she said, "but I still had time for my friends." She skated, she went to school, but she made sure she enjoyed herself, too. "She's fun-loving," said her mother, Pat. "She loves to have fun and live life to its fullest." The toughest part for Lipinski was being away from her father. "That was hard," she said. "I missed him so much, but I got to go home occasionally and see him."

*Lipinski receives a hug as her coach Richard Callaghan looks on. She had just won the gold medal at U.S. Figure Skating Championships. Febuary 15, 1997.*

## U.S.A. WORLD CHAMPION

Before she reached her teens, Lipinski was already one of the top figure skaters in the United States. When she was 14, she won not only the 1997 U.S. championships, but also the world title in the same year. She was the youngest skater ever to claim both the U.S. and world championships. In late 1997, the U.S. Olympic Committee chose Lipinski as its Sports Woman of the Year. She was the youngest ever to receive that award. "It's such a great honor," she said. "Of all the sports people in the U.S., I got picked. It just feels really good."

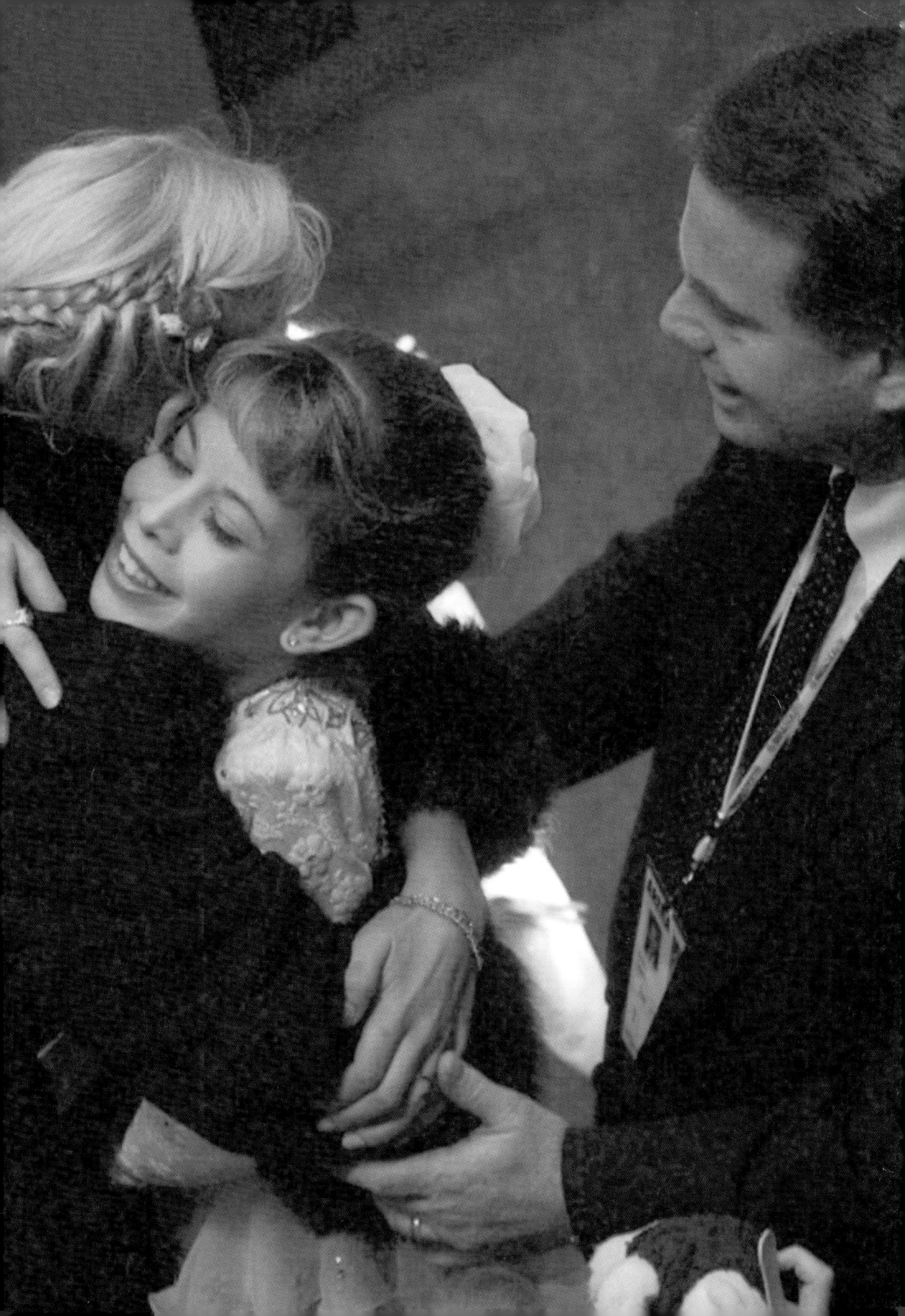

*Lipinski performs during an exhibition following the U.S. Figure Skating Championships. January 11, 1998. She placed second and was named to the U.S. Olympic team.*

In January 1998, Lipinski and Kwan battled in the U.S. championships. Lipinski skated well, but Kwan, the 1996 U.S. and world champion, was unbelievable. Many of the judges gave Kwan perfect scores of 6.0. Lipinski wound up second. Both skaters qualified for the Olympics, but Kwan was now the clear favorite. As it turned out, finishing second at the U.S. championships might have been the best thing to happen to Lipinski. Kwan, and not Lipinski, was now expected to win the gold—and that was fine with Lipinski. "I like to be the underdog," she said.

## 80-POUND WONDER

Lipinski went to the Nagano Olympic Games with one goal: to have fun. No matter what else happened, she wanted to enjoy her Olympic experience. She marched in the opening ceremonies. She lived in the Olympic Village and sent e-mail to other athletes. She got hockey

19

star Wayne Gretzky's autograph. And she hung around with sumo wrestling champion Akebono. The 516-pound Akebono joked to the 80-pound Lipinski that his calf was bigger than she was. Lipinski also watched the men's figure skating competition, rooting for American Todd Eldredge.

*Lipinski spins during her short program at the World Figure Skating Championships in Lausanne, Switzerland. March 21, 1997.*

## COMPETING AT LAST

When it was finally time for Lipinski to skate her short program, the first part of the competition, she felt no pressure. "The Olympics are very stressful," she said. "I just told myself to try to have fun and forget everything else. When I got on the ice, it was like I knew what the Olympics are about. I had that feeling of pure joy." When she finished her short program, she looked as if she had that feeling. Lipinski had skated well, but Kwan had skated a little better. Kwan led after the short program, but even so, Lipinski was happy with her performance.

U.S.A 's Lipinski kisses her gold medal after winning the ladies free skating long program in Nagano, Japan. Fellow American Michelle Kwan took the silver, and China's Lu Chen, the bronze. Febuary 20, 1998.

Lipinski was even happier after skating her long program a few days later. "I felt this was one of the best programs I've ever done," she said after winning the gold medal. "I've been training hard and skating great, but when I went out there, it just all happened." "Tara had the magic," said Rosalynn Sumners, the 1984 Olympic silver medalist. "She had the Olympic magic moment so many of us dreamt of." It was a moment Lipinski had first dreamt of 13 years before. That night, she went to sleep with the gold medal still around her neck—"just to make sure it was there," she said. Yes, it was there. And, yes, some dreams do come true.